Moments

From the Book of Life

By Harvey J. Sullivan

Dorrance Publishing Co
585 Alpha Drive
Pittsburgh, PA 15238
Visit our website at www.dorrancebookstore.com

ISBN: 979-8-88729-276-2
eISBN: 979-8-88729-776-7

Moments

From the Book of Life

How can it be that only a few days have passed,
The clock ticks, the calendar changes… it's a new day at last
Eyes wide open that were once full of tears
Hope overtakes, where before only doubt appeared.

One might think it's impossible for this all to be true
But the impossible became possible the moment I met you
Since that day, since that time, since the moment our eyes met
In that instance everything changed, a change that I love…
    no fears… no regrets.

Words are sometimes all I have, to express just how I feel
Sometimes words don't seem like enough; but in a word this is
    all very real
I've been touched by an angel, and though it's only been a few
    days
How do I love this angel… let me count the ways.

I spend my days dreaming… thinking about the moments that
we've shared
Thinking about your smile, your laughter… and how good it
feels to have someone that cares
I dream. I think. I anticipate, like a kid, what the next day will
bring
Knowing that the next moment will be richer, fuller, in a
word…it will be amazing.

Shut up for so long, have been these feelings inside
They are now bursting out, full throttle, unafraid, no longer do
they hide
The sun shines bright just like every day before
But yet it's brighter, warmer, more beautiful… it, like you, I
simply adore

In everything I see now, somehow it reminds me of you
With every heartbeat I feel, I now feel the power of two
Two hearts beating as one, our minds seemingly in rhythm from
the start
Your beauty, your touch… everything you do and are, has cap-
tured my heart.

There were times when I've been in the pit… wondering if I'd
    ever come out
Feelings so low, feeling all alone… all I wanted to do was shout
Shout, scream, cry… the emotions were so very strong
Make the hurt stop… make the pain stop… it's all so wrong

But. One day came a voice, and it came just for me
It said, "Don't give up hope… rise up… believe!"
It let me know that I was never alone… that things would be
    alright
The voice gave me hope, it gave me peace, it stayed with me
    throughout the night

And now I see what the voice knew well in advance
The voice loved me, it strengthened me… it gave me a second
    chance
Now, when you speak, I hear that voice… it penetrates my soul
Your voice, it soothes me, it draws me in… what the voice has
    given me I never want to let go.

With my eyes closed, I can see you, you're a vision, a master-
 piece, a pure visual delight
I feel you, deep inside, I feel your smile, it shines so bright
With my eyes closed, I sense you, you are so very near
You're right here, in my arms, with my eyes closed it's so very
 clear

Where were you... all those days and nights when life just
 seemed a continuous pain
When it seemed always dreary, when the days were full of rain
You were right there, closing in, but yet so far away
You were making your way to me, and I to you, you were slowly
 on your way

Life happens, but no regrets do I have for the experiences I've
 had
For they shaped me, they taught me, in fact they freed me...
 even when bad
Today I can say it's all been worth it... I'm happy and it's clear
 to see
Those experiences were priceless... and a start to a whole new
 me

It's another day, another flight, another trip I must make
One more taxi, one more runway, one more ascension to take
Like this trip, my life has journey after journey been
You come, you go, you regroup… and you do it all over again

At 30,000 feet, all you can see seems vast yet small
From that vantage point, you wonder if you matter at all
How important can you be… this thought comes and goes
At 30,000 feet, lots of questions… is anyone else out there?
    Who knows

Then, suddenly, your mind shifts… because there's someone
    special that takes your breath away
You think about this special someone, their smile, you start to
    dream about the days
Now you're beside me, my companion, just for me your arms
    are open wide
It's not just another day, it's a moment, and the thought of the
    moment brings extreme pleasure on this particular airplane
    ride

Feelings. Such a small word, yet sometimes looms large over
   one's life
Sometimes held in check... other times out of control; some-
   times joy; sometimes strife
Even the most capable speaker can at times struggle to describe
The range of emotions, the pain, the hurt... the battle inside

But there are sometimes chance meetings, you didn't see com-
   ing your way
And that moment excites you, it ignites you, it totally makes
   your day
Of course, it's not the moment, it's something more significant
   taking place
Feelings of love are now sprouting up in what was once an
   empty space

You don't worry, you don't fear, you don't run away and hide
You embrace it, you embrace this feeling in every way...taking
   it all in stride
You feel alive; it all seems unimaginable... too good to be true
Not only is it too good, it's amazing, it's awesome; I love the
   feelings now... and I love that they are only for you

In spite of my past, in spite of my pain, in my life I've been in-
    credibly blessed
I give all praise to God, for He alone got me through my mess
Things were supposed to last forever; it wasn't supposed to just
    end this way…
But because it did, I continually spoke to my Heavenly Father.
    I cried. I prayed.

Look forward to now; today; the present is here
I'm stronger, I'm better, I'm unbreakable and yet this one thing
    is clear
If it had not been for the things that I thought went wrong
I'd still be stuck in that dysfunction… but thank God there's a
    new song

The song starts with my heartbeat… so strong, so proud, so
    loud
The chorus is like the chirp of the birds, chest out… all proud
Inside there's a solo… yes, let love have its way
That solo is for you; it's about your beauty, your touch, your
    lips, and the way you sway

Not a lot of time has passed from then until now
Yet it seems like a lifetime, and you wonder how
How blessed I am that you are there for me
I'm blessed beyond measure to have someone like you love me

Windows. Sometimes they allow us in, give us all access to
what's inside
Yet, windows don't reveal everything, some things we don't see
because, from the inside – windows they hide
You sometimes only see what you look for, on the surface is
where we gaze
Yet if you were to look deeper, inside, at what you found; you'd
be amazed

There's always more to see, if you'd only use your eyes
If you'd just look deeper, at the heart, I believe you'd be sur-
prised
When you look beyond the obvious, when you look into those
eyes
You'd discover wonder, you'd see deep beauty, you'd experience
God's great prize

That great prize is the person you are, the special soul, magnif-
icent, what more can I say
I see you, inside, deep; yes, you're beautiful… but in a much
deeper way
You're an experience, a dream come true, words cannot describe
all that you are
But as l look out the window, I see it, and it captures you… you
are most definitely a star

The man I am may not be the man you see
The man I am runs deep, so you'd have to look beyond the surface to truly understand me
And while understanding is welcomed, there's still more to reveal
The man I am, has been shaped by life… with lots of layers for you to peel

Like a diamond shaped by pressure, life has done the same for me
Deeply rooted and grounded in faith, and the gentle love that my mother provided was key
The man I am, has been tossed, blown, kicked…yet I'm standing strong like a tree
Faith, love, and hard work are my pillars of strength; in them I believe

The man I am is not the man I was, but some choose not to forget
The man I am, can now look back over his life and experience no regrets
The man that I am is the man I am with you
The man that I am… has an amazing love in his life, the man I am… has a dream come true

Week after week, it's the same... get packed... get to the air-
    port... go fly
I look for the same seat, Exit Row; I look out the window...I
    see the stars in the sky
And often I dream, I think, I wonder about the day gone by
I think and I search... I'm looking for an answer to the ques-
    tion... "why?'

Before the answer comes, I look out at the sky once more
Now the question "why?" is replaced, it's now the answer to
    "how?" that I'm now looking for
In reality, the answer will likely change, because change is oc-
    curring in you
Nothing stays the same, change will come no matter what you
    do

It doesn't seem to matter as I look at the stars... they continue
    to shine bright
Through all the years, through all the storms, come what may
    or what might
When you know who you are, and the purpose for which you
    were placed in the sky
You too will not only have the strength to do so, but a reason
    to rise!

There are times when life seems so hard, it just doesn't seem
    fair
It can all feel overwhelming, it can feel like nothing is right, and
    that no one cares
But in my years of living, I've discovered that life has its' certain
    truths
One lasting lesson I've learned is that no matter what... there's
    no one more important than you

You are important! That is a fact and it cannot be denied
You deserve to be loved, you deserve to be happy; this despite
    all the lonely nights you've cried
You've had to overcome so many things... and some that ripped
    you apart inside
You've had to make it, step by step, day by day, even when the
    hurt and pain you had to hide

You knew a new day would come, that your best was on the way
You knew there was love, an angel, a sweet soul out there for
    you... that would take your breath away
Your heart never wavered, it beat strong and with a purpose all
    the day long
Your heart knew, even if you didn't, that there'd be someone
    special for you...now beside you, and together creating a
    beautiful new song

Happiness…it's a word that is sometimes hard to describe
We all have an idea of what it is, we feel like we know its' vibe
Yet happiness isn't always what it may appear to be
Sometimes happiness is a mask, hiding the real you so no one
    can see

Happiness sometimes makes visits, and may not stay for long
Or it may stay for a while, then other times just for the length
    of a certain song
It's not that happiness doesn't want to last
Rather, it's sometimes interrupted by others, yet other times by
    your past

But the day will come when happiness, in you, will come alive
While before you've only been getting by, the time is coming
    for you to thrive
Happiness has been fighting, pushing to get where you are
Happiness doesn't quit, it never gives up, it would climb the
    highest mountain to find you… there's no distance too far

I pray that happiness has found its way to you.

Have you ever wanted to be loved, even if for a day or a night?
Have you wished and dreamed of a storybook love, wondering
    what that would be like?
Have you thirsted just for a prince or princess to come steal
    your heart?
Have you cried at night because your reality and your dreams
    were so far apart?

If you've shed tears, hurt, and despair… then to you I say cry
    no more
Love is coming to you, not riding a white horse… just simply
    walking through your door
What door you may ask; and if that's your question, then let me
    be clear
Love is about to hold your hand, kiss your cheek, and nibble on
    your ear

Love has been there all along, but it needed to be revived
It's been in every inch of your body; it's been there all along…
    inside

May love cause you to take flight and soar like never before.

Choices. We make them all the time, yet how do we know for
sure

Which choice is best for us? Which will cost us the least con-
cern? Which will cost more?

How can we know when from the start it looks so clear…

Yet, later or what's worse, even sooner… our choices we'll begin
to fear

You see, some choices we make are not solely for us… others
are involved

At times choices are easy, simple, leaving you with a feeling of
'problem solved'

Yet at other times these same choices can turn your entire world
upside down

Leaving you to wonder, 'how did this happen?' 'what do I do
now?'

Breath. Don't panic. Whatever the situation, make a choice to
make it through the day

Choose to lean on your faith. Choose to do what you can…
choose to pray!

Recognize that sometimes we make choices without having all
the facts

We make choices sometimes with our hearts… or our heads…
other times we just react

We react to what we feel, or see, or hear – based on where we
are today
We cannot predict or see into the future… come what will or
may
Choices sometimes seem to take on a life of their own
Therefore, just know that a choice that seemed right today…
can still go so wrong

It's a new year, the calendar has changed, and hope and energy
are all around
Energy to set and achieve new goals, hope that this year will be
full of ups… no downs!
We believe in our hearts that better days are on the way…
We believe that with the change of the calendar, all issues and
challenges ended with the close of yesterday

If only it were that simple… if only we could change the broken
pieces of our lives with such ease
If only we could erase sickness, hurt, pain, our tears… if only
we could… can we, please!
No, in life our days and our nights play out right before our
eyes
Some things we can see coming, but others will catch us by sur-
prise

Even so, always remember there's a power that lives inside of
you
And while it's a new day and a new year, this power has been
there from the beginning… He's been bringing you
through
Through what? All things! Whether you were aware or not
He; God… He's been there for you… and He promised He
won't stop!

When you don't know what to do, God will get you through.

What kind of man am I? This is not a question I thought would
be on my mind…
But, for some reason, today it is… so let me answer the ques-
tion; allow me this time
First, I will say, that I am a man; this is no excuse, but fact…
and one I express with pride
As a man I stand, front and center, upright, no shame. As a man
I will not hide.

I'm a man that gives, provides, and cares for the blessings I've
been given
As a man, I take responsibility; grinding daily and working my
ass off to make an honest living
I'm a man that doesn't take… I choose to earn it; if not, then
I'm a man that can do without
I'm a man that wants to owe no one, I'm a man that stands with
God; He has my back… no doubt

I'm a man that thinks, feels, and expresses himself in a respectful
way
However, having said that… I'm no pushover… don't make that
mistake today
I will do for most, all that I can, expecting nothing in return
For in the end, I'm a man… born in love, refined by fire…
so if and when I'm knocked down… I'll get up, because
that's the man I've been since the day I was born

We all have opportunities to live, to love, and to know what it's
like to reach for the stars
We can dream big dreams, we can visit places near or far
We can smile, we can laugh, or we can cry… and sometimes all
within the same day
We have the opportunity to live our lives, the way that we want,
regardless of what others have to say

What we do with our opportunities is where the difference be-
gins to show
Some will make the absolute most of theirs… but then others…
only God knows
But if by chance you've been given this day, then there's hope
that you'll be the one
The one that will turn their opportunity into gold… and a suc-
cessful race you'll run

Let no one kill the dreams that are bursting with excitement
inside you each day
Let no one's negative words take root; let no one's jealousy get
in your way
Be the one that makes it despite the limits or challenges you'll
constantly face
You've been built for this; you've been set apart and blessed; so
carry on; what God has for you IS FOR YOU… get to work
my child… God says "Take your place!"

One of the hardest things to do in life… is to forgive
Even though we know it's right… some things, it seems, we
    want to hold onto for as long as we live
We know we must let go, and though it seems that easy… we
    all know that it's not
But if we don't forgive, if we hold onto the hurt, we'll be forever
    stuck in that spot

So, forgive… let go… don't let this thing linger another day
For forgiveness is as much for you as it is for them… forgive-
    ness will bring you peace – peace not for a moment… but
    peace that stays
You see, it no longer matters what was done, or said… that's all
    in the past
What matters now is that you're free of it all, it's power or hold
    on you no longer last

So, in forgiving, remember to also forgive yourself
We're human, we make mistakes… at times we turn right, only
    to find the correct path was to the left
Believe that good is coming, not just for you, but for any that
    your forgiveness is targeted to
And then live, don't look back, look to the hills, and allow for-
    giveness to do its wonderous, marvelous healing work in
    you

Dreams. We all have them, whether it be during the day, or late at night

We dream sometimes of amazing things, then wonder if they'll come true... hoping they might

We close our eyes, or other times dreams come to us when we're wide awake

Sometimes our dreams can be so odd, it makes us wonder... was it something I ate?

Sometimes our dreams are in response to something that's real

We dream of better days, a better life, a dream that takes away the pain we feel

Or perhaps, it's a dream born out of joy, perhaps a day like no other before

We pause, we think, we recall that feeling and we dream of having it more

Inside of you are dreams, many of which are waiting to come true

You see, when you dream there are no limits... it's when you awake that it's all up to you

You have the gift, the Great Provider... and He's promised to be with you for life

So don't just dream... but DO dream, and when you wake up just know "I can do all things through Christ"

Dream Big Dreams.

Have you ever had the experience where your house was not a
home?
By that, I mean, that in spite of everything or everyone there…
you still felt alone
Seemingly all that you need should have been inside, just be-
hind the doors
But it was just a house, for now… yet you wished it was much
more

People may drive by, they'll notice your address
What they can't see from their view, is that inside this house it's
a mess!
You see, your house sometimes needs cleaning from the inside
out
So right here, understand that your physical address is not what
I'm talking about

You, my friend, are a dwelling, a home to the Most High
So some things inside your 'house' must go… some things must
die!
Home is where the heart is… this will always be true
When your house becomes a home, you'll feel so much
better… you'll be at peace, at home, knowing God loves
you.

Life… it has moments that make you pause
There are waves of moments that deserve our applause
Special blessings, memories, minutes that take our breath away
These can all change in a flash… so let's always be thankful for
today

Today is what you have after yesterday slipped into the past
Today is your now, and from experience we know that like yes-
terday, today won't last
Soon today will do the same, like the days before, it's light will
fade away
So, be sure to take this day in… this day is your today!

Today is your now… be sure your eyes, heart, arms, ears, and
mind are open to what it will bring
Will you miss its blessings because you were looking for some
other thing?
The moments will come, and be right there for you to put in
your bank
Today is your now… today – to you I say "Thanks!"

Today do something; say something; make someone's today
memorable
No matter what, always remember that you're "enjoy – able!"
Today is your now, don't let 'this' today pass
Take a moment; breath it in; smile… make today special… and
watch how it lasts!

Have you ever wished you could be inside someone's head?
Just for a moment to discover what makes them tick, what
　　things they like… what things they dread
The mind is a terrible thing to waste; this was said years ago
What amazing things are inside there, taking root, ready to ex-
　　plode?

Of course, before others, it's our own heads we must first master
For surely with our minds, we've done some good, yet other
　　times… disaster
There's so much to stimulate your mind, so we must be careful
　　what we take in
For greatness, success, and prosperity lay between your ears…
　　don't ever doubt you can win!

Do not give ear to the noise or hate that will surely come your
　　way
Just keep working, keep believing, your breakthrough could
　　come today!
Fill your mind with positive thoughts, words, and a song…
And before you know it… from your head will come greatness.
　　Trust and believe; it won't be long.

To everything there is a season, yes the bible makes that clear
But what exactly does that mean for me… what things are waiting for me in this new year?
I don't have that answer, not yet, so I must keep moving forward… this I know
And like the seasons, from Winter, to Fall, to Spring, and Summer… all around us new things will grow

A season can represent a certain or specific moment in time
It may not be physical or literal… it could merely be a change in our mind
A season could represent that the time is coming… that your day of rejoicing is on the way
It can signal that the cold, the clouds, and the storms in your life have all rolled away

So, like a farmer, be busy getting your soil in good shape
For we all know that preparation is key… none of this will happen by mistake
In life our seasons can last for just a moment, or far as long as God allows
This season could be your best ever, so be prepared to be blessed… not only later; but right now!

It's your season.

There were days in the not-so-distant past, where I wondered,
"why is this happening… is this going to last?"
I'm sure we've all had days like this, where we sometimes dread
just getting out of bed
We feel like we have nothing to look forward to… either real
or in our heads

And, then, sometimes suddenly, things begin to turn around
Your spirits are lifted, all that had you down now is in the distant
past… a smile now replaces your frown
There is a new hope, a new reason to feel like you matter once
again
There's someone in your life now that makes the moments
meaningful… all you can do is grin

You see, not so long ago you could only dream of the day when
loves' power would grip you tight
When the energy from being loved and cared for would take
hold of you, and keep you by day and by night
This is not made up, or make believe, you know deep inside
that it's real
You now have no fear, you now only anticipate each day, know-
ing and making sure that special someone knows exactly
how you feel

I think most can relate to becoming comfortable with things
    we later questioned
We were so caught up in the moment or the struggle, that we
    didn't notice things changed... or when
We tend to get used to things, and then at times we become
    numb
Then all of a sudden, or so it seems, our eyes are opened, and
    at that moment our first reaction is to run

Typically, when we think of running, it's as in 'running away'
But indirectly when that occurs, you start running to some-
    thing... even on that very same day
You determine to escape, to start anew, to live, and discover the
    fullness and your purpose yet to be fulfilled
You see things differently now, possibilities seem limitless, you
    realize you're not an empty vessel... you have so much
    more to give

And now, you have new, fresh and wonderful experiences...
    many of the hurts of the past have been replaced
And as more beautiful experiences are sure to come... some
    may even be erased
You're free now, no longer a prisoner to one's idea of who you
    are
You're free, totally free... live, love, laugh, and shine... you're
    precious; you're strong; you're loved. You're my shining
    star.

Sometimes the events of life can be hard to understand
How one day everything is good, and the next day you're hang-
    ing by a strand
Yes, one day you're up and everything is going your way
Then, all of a sudden, life; it happens, and you're left speechless,
    not knowing what to say

If this has been your life, to you I say, "hope is making a house
    call to you today"
Hope is knocking, ringing your bell, standing there… hope
    wants to pray.
You see, hope knows your name, hope knows your story well
Hope has fresh air for you, new life, and there's so much more
    to tell

Hope says "No Matter What" don't ever quit on yourself
Hope says "Hold on to Me" even when it seems like there's
    nothing left
You see my friend, hope has always been there, even through
    the darkest of times
And hope is here even stronger now… hope from on high, like
    the bright sunshine

Even when you don't have hope, hope has you! Don't ever give
    up… hope strong!

Over the years you learn you can be happy with less than you
thought
You can be fulfilled and have joy… not dependent on the things
you've bought
You can have genuine satisfaction, and a smile that's sincere and
true
Not because of things, but because of the maturity inside you

Things will at some point mean less as time passes by
Some, even though you've treasured them, they will only so
often now catch your eye
This is why having someone to love adds such richness to your
days
Someone that you love, and they love you back with a love that
doesn't fade away

Things get old or outdated, and they soon lose their appeal
Love, on the other hand, gets stronger… I'm talking about a
love that's real
Love grows, it blooms, it lifts you in every way
I have that love, and I get that love back, and I look forward to
us sharing that love every single day

Things matter less when you know it's not the 'things' that
matter.

Sometimes we get so busy, so caught up with just trying to make
a living
We fight through issues, go through challenges… it seems like
we're always giving
And there are days where it all seems to come together
But then far too many days you wonder if the present will be
your forever

Challenges and issues… overcoming them is what strengthens
you
You are great and magnificent… no one can do what you do
Not everyone in your life is for your success, sad but true
But even this works in your favor, because God Almighty will
see you through

Don't be afraid, and don't worry over things lost
Sometimes holding onto things that you shouldn't is a far
greater cost
In all that you do, guard your heart, and 'to thyself be true'
You don't need all that you thought; you making it – that all
starts with you

You're powerful, you're strong, you're smart… true, true, and
true!
So let loose and let the greatest love fill you and let that same
love flow from you.

Do you ever wonder or think back on how easy life was as a
kid?
How it seemed not to matter, whether this or that you did
How the days didn't really matter because all you did was
play…
And you could play, even if you didn't have toys… you could
still play all day

You see, as a kid, all of your basic needs were met
You didn't have the worries of your parents – because we
weren't grownups yet
You couldn't wait to get older, to do things like have your own
money…maybe a house
As a kid you would dream those big expensive dreams… about
everything… even a spouse

It wasn't easy because you were a kid… it was easy because you
had no worries
It's sad how that thinking has changed… how becoming an
adult changed the story
It'd be great to play outside again; all day and night until the
streetlights came on
But it all changed, or has it? Are those kid-like days really gone?

I challenge you to find the kid in you today
I challenge you to find him/her and let them loose… let them
play all night and all day!

I want to speak this truth, for only your ears to hear
This is something I feel you should know, something you've
    needed to know for years
It's important that you know there's no one in the world just
    like you…
No one, nowhere, no how… you, and you alone are the one and
    only you

So, what's so special about you? Don't you dare to ask
If I could I'd take you back… back to the day God put love to
    task
You are a masterpiece, a gift, a jewel, straight from the Master's
    hand
You were no accident, you were/are intentional… you are part
    of the Master's plan

You are unique, amazing, and beautiful, and there's no other
    anywhere like you
The way you look, the way you speak, walk… only you can do
    and be you….
By His hands you were shaped, and He has even bigger plans
    for you now
You are fabulous, you are mighty… just say "I am!"; don't ask
    'how?'

33

Believe in you; believe that you're the apple of God's eye
Believe in His perfect love for you... believe that for you
   He died
But dead no longer... nor should your dreams go unfilled
Why?... because you believe; and because He lives!

There are times that I sit, and allow my mind to travel in space
Not knowing where it's going to take me; to what time? To
what place?
My mind enjoys being free to go from here to there
It stops along the way, revealing glimpses of past times shared

There's my mother, sitting on the porch snapping peas or
shucking corn
She's the sweetest woman I've ever known... I was fortunate to
her to be born
She was the rock, and she gave us all so much love
And she's doing today what she's always done... only now it's
from heaven above

My dad, my brother Ed, and mama Cloretta... your faces are
all so clear
You were each special and significant... my mind keeps you
each so near
I'm the little kid from Nicholas Street... my mind continuously
reminds me of that
I'm thankful for these moments, and that for just an instance,
my mind can take me back

Sometimes we have to be reminded that we have plenty of rea-
sons to smile
We get so caught up in the day to day, not realizing how far
we've come… all the while
It's likely not been super easy, in fact it may have been a strug-
gle… and that's ok
Because no matter the situation, you're still here today

I believe! I believe great blessings are coming your way
You may have heard this before, but even so… please hear what
I say
There's a plan and a purpose that only you can fulfill
I believe you're strong, powerful, and mighty… and achieve this
purpose you will!

You're a beautiful diamond, a star… you're 24K gold!
You don't have to apologize, you're a child of God… claim it
and be bold!
Move forward, step by step, for reverse is not a gear that you
know
With every breath you take, purpose, positivity, and passion are
saying, "Come on now… you go!"

Never give up… there's no quit.

Today you need to know that everything will be alright
Despite the heartache, bad breaks… there are new blessings
    coming into sight
Just know that the pain, the tears, the doubts – are all passing
    away
The storm is over, you'll breathe anew… please hear what I say

Life hasn't been perfect, not for you… in fact, it's been tough
I can imagine there have been days when you've thought
    'enough is enough!'
But suddenly from out of nowhere, Hope is moving in
And Hope brings company… Faith and Love are Hopes'
    friends

So now you have an army to help fight for the cause
This army has never lost a battle, they fight non-stop; there's
    no pause
What you thought was not possible, suddenly has changed right
    before your eyes
Hope, Faith, and Love are undefeated… you're being restored;
    your enemies are stunned and surprised

When you can do nothing, just hold on my friend
Joy will come… just keep holding on tightly, with all your
    strength until then
I'm telling you what I know from my own experiences in life…
    not just something I've heard
When you can't trust anything else, you can always trust in His
    word!

She was my sister, yet so much more
She was an angel that I'm forever grateful for
She was a gift, to me, and to so many she gave
She was a light; in and through her, God's goodness she gave

Her voice was strong… a powerful testimony she shared
Her voice brought tears of joy, it lifted you out of despair
Precious Lord; Amazing Grace; On Christ the Solid Rock I
    Stand…
She sang us all happy… both at home and across the land

Darphine, even now, I can hear you and it makes me glad
I'll cry, I'll be sorry, but because of your spirit I won't be sad
I'll be thankful that God blessed my life, giving me such a
    strong example of grace
You, your life, your words, your smile… all are now welcomed
    in His heavenly place

You gave us all you had… and we'll miss you for sure
I love you, my dear sister, and I know there's a great celebration
    awaiting you as you walk through Heaven's door

RIH.